SCHIRMER'S LIBRARY
OF MUSICAL CLASSICS

Vol. 1358

ROBERT SCHUMANN

Op. 54

Concerto

In A minor

For the Piano

With the Orchestral Accompaniment
Arranged for a Second Piano

Edited by
EDWIN HUGHES

✿

G. SCHIRMER, Inc.

DISTRIBUTED BY
HAL•LEONARD®
CORPORATION
7777 W. BLUEMOUND RD. P.O. BOX 13819 MILWAUKEE, WI 53213

Concerto

Dedicated to Ferdinand Hiller

Composed in 1841 (first movement), and 1845 (second and third movements); published in August, 1846

Edited by
Edwin Hughes

R. Schumann. Op. 54

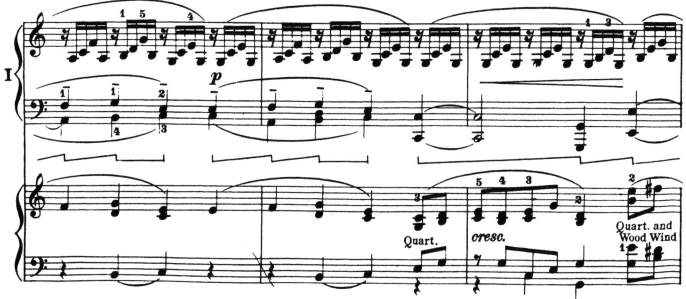

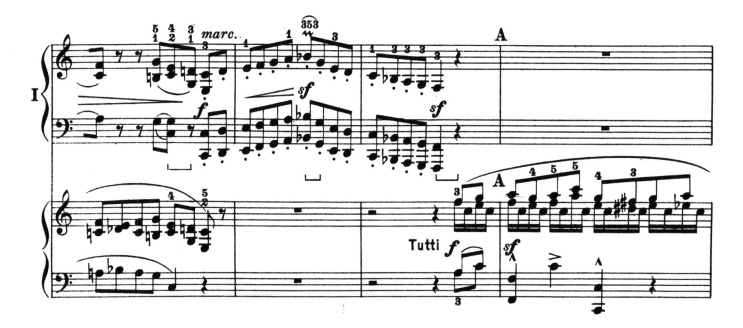

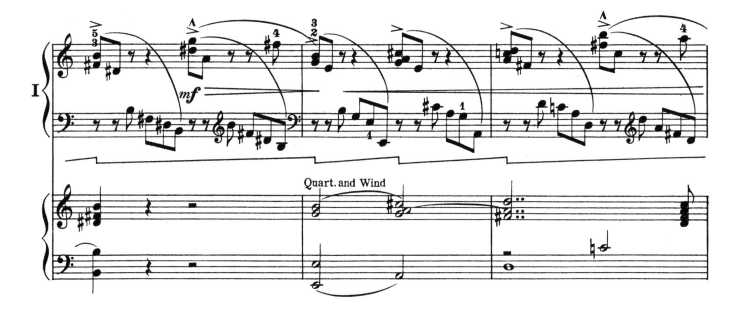

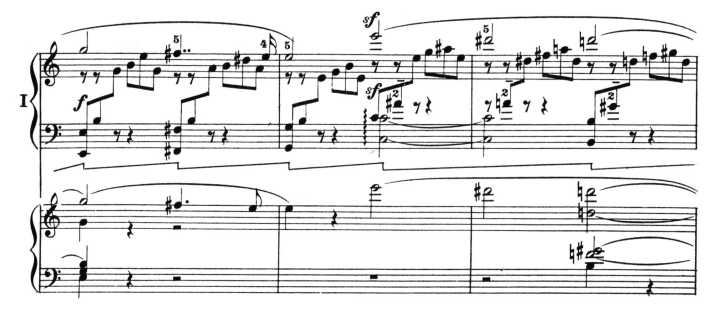

sempre dim.

Timp.

D Tempo I°

D Tempo I°

Tutti

Wind
p espress.

sf

Solo

p espress.

sf

Quart.

p

pizz.

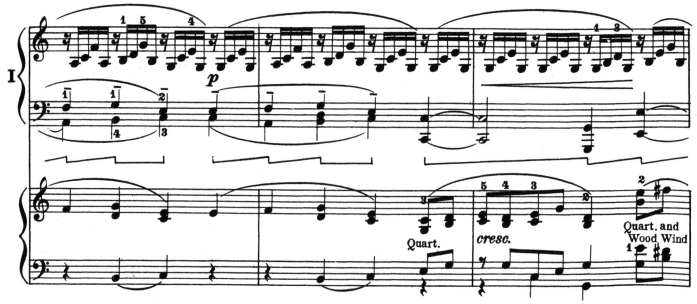

Vcello arco

Animato

Animato
Clar.
Quart.

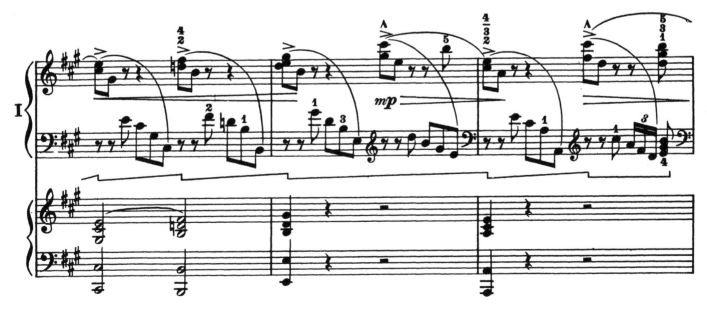

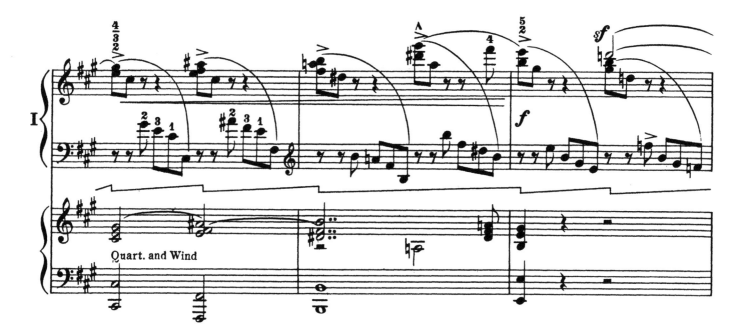

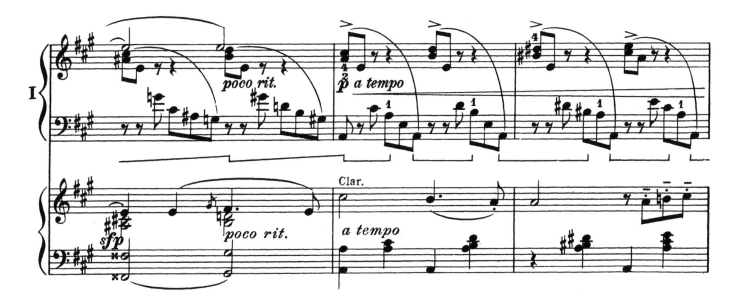

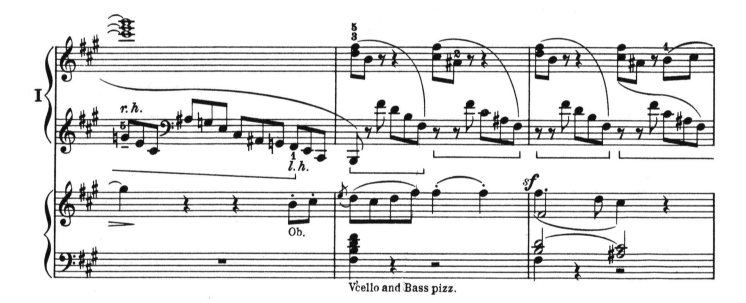

Vcello and Bass pizz.

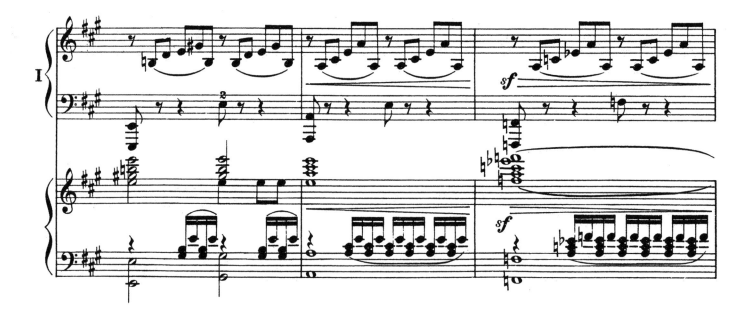

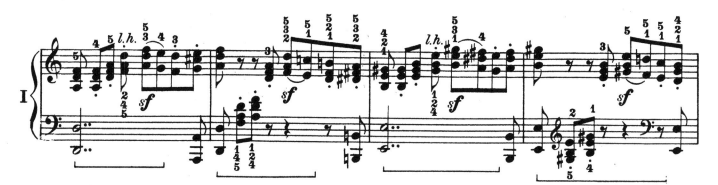

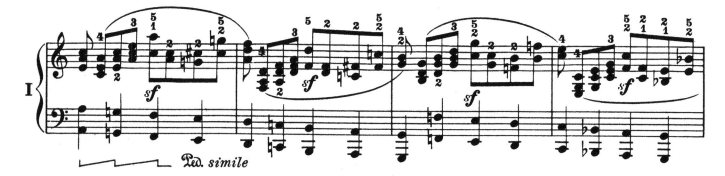

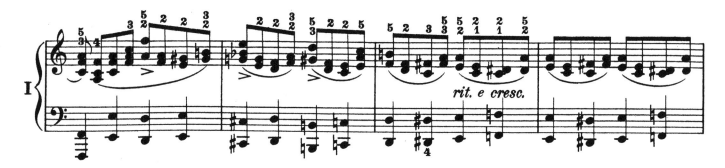

Un poco andante

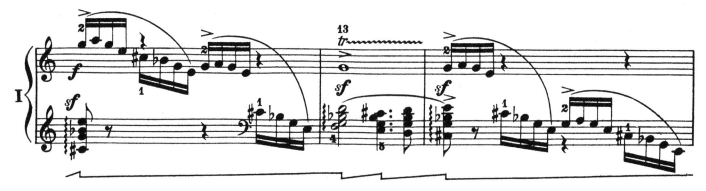

I Allegro molto ($\textit{d}$ = 88)

I Allegro molto

p Quart. and Wood Wind

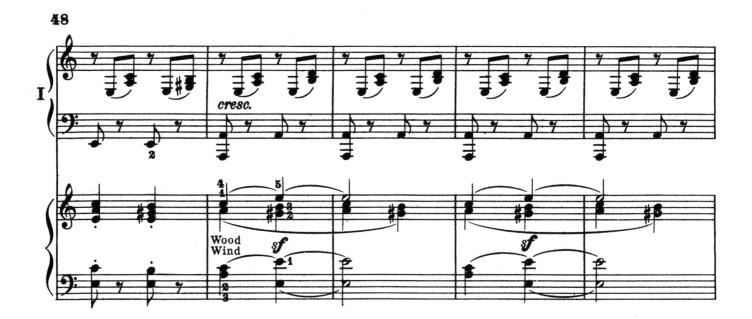

Intermezzo
Andante grazioso (♪ = 120)

Viola and V'cello

Bass and Bassoon

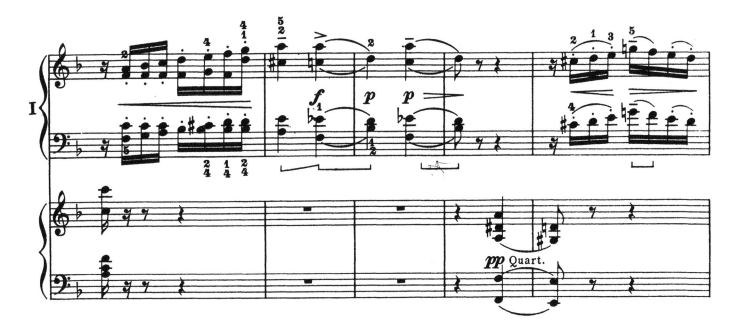

Allegro vivace (♩. = 80)

Allegro vivace (♩. = 80)

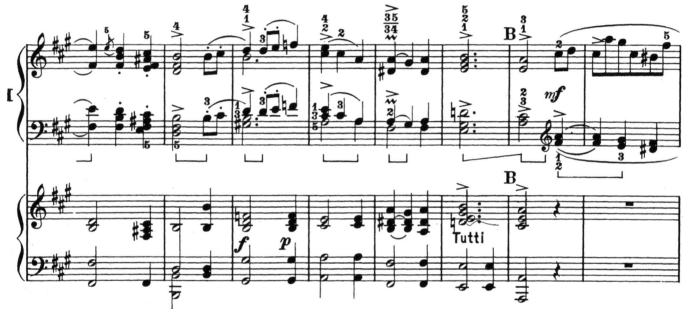

una corda

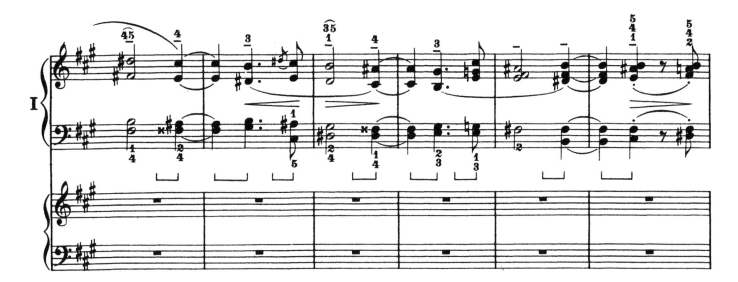

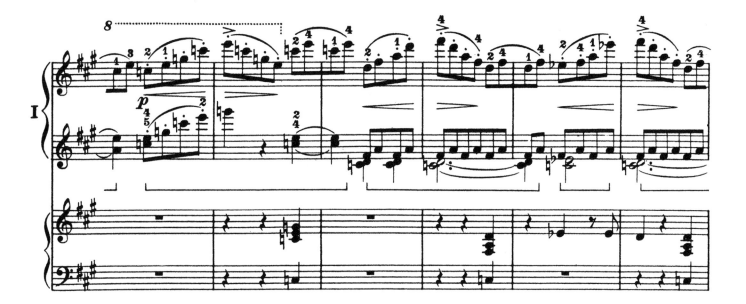

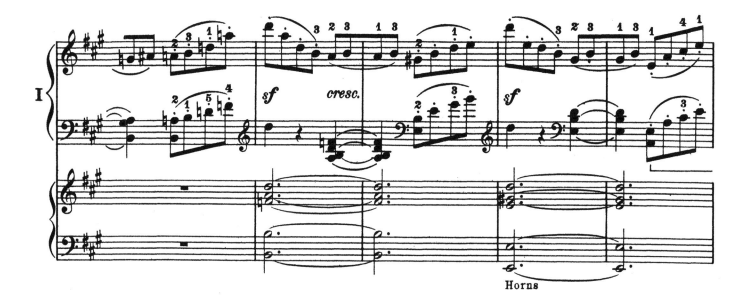

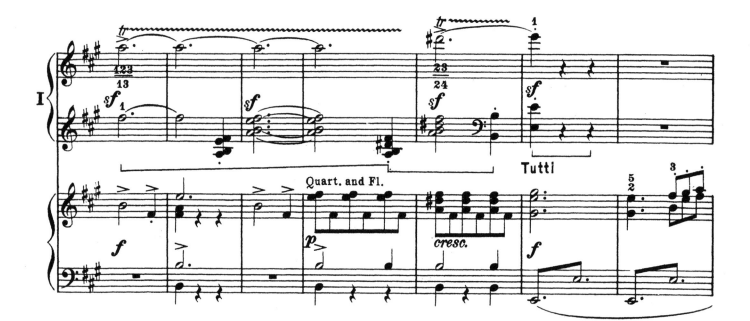

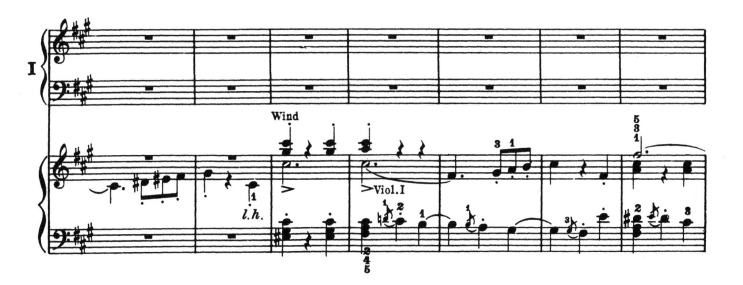

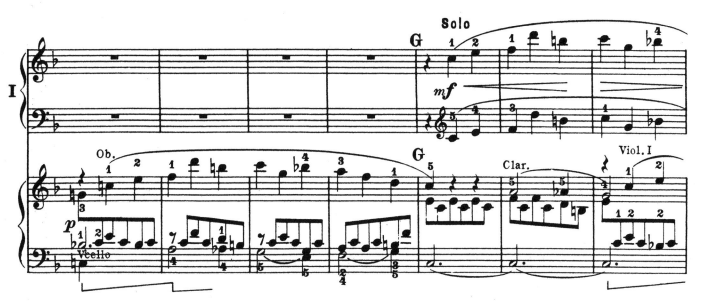

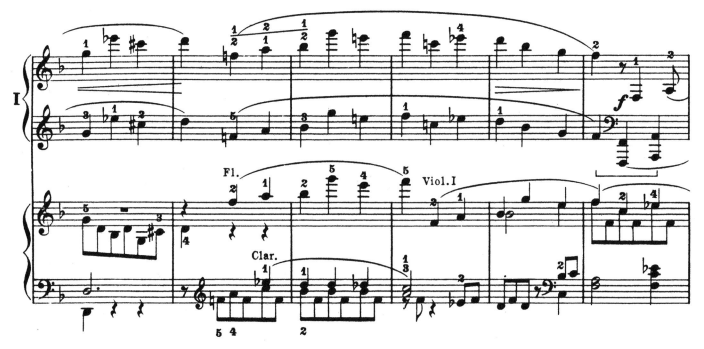

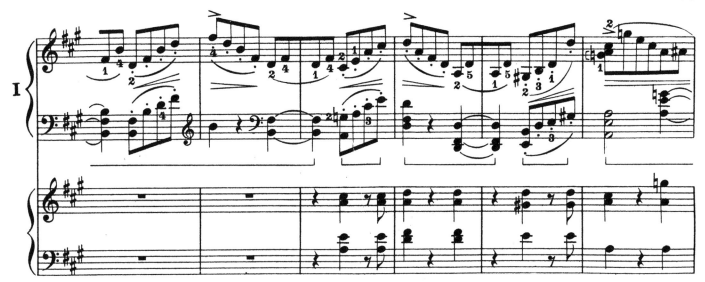

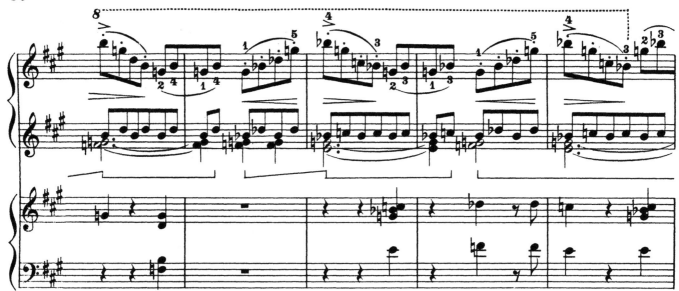

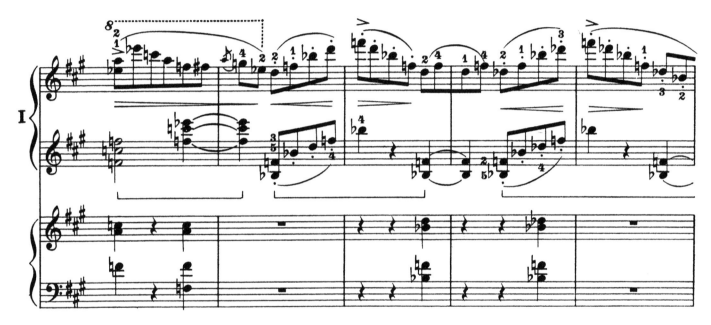

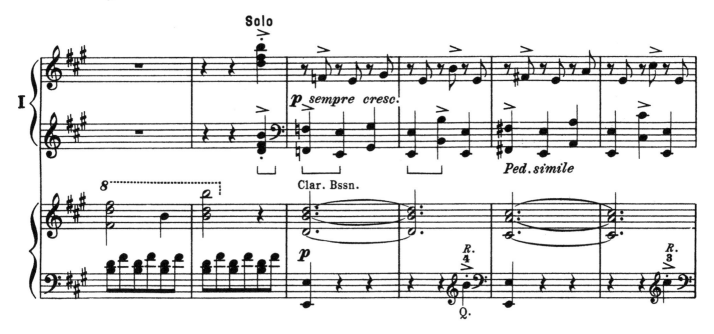

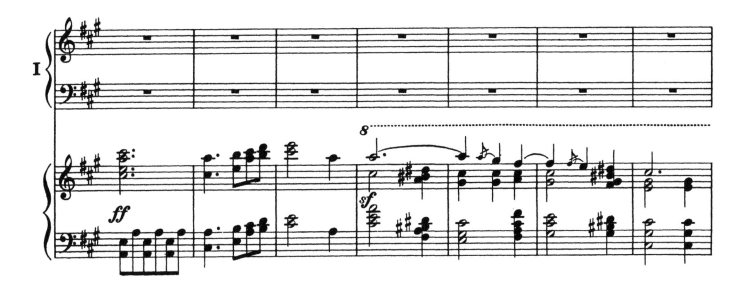

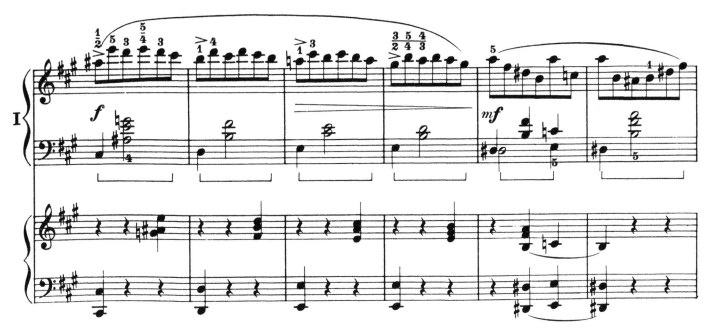

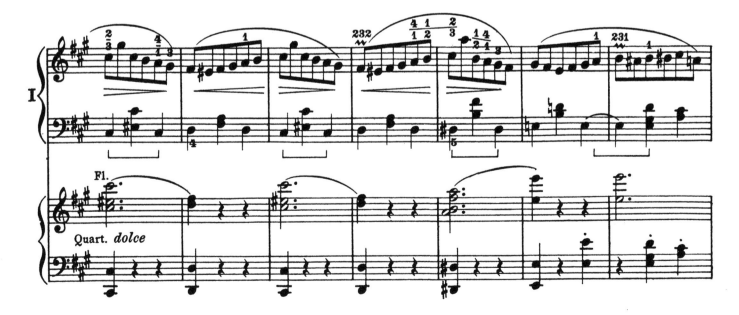

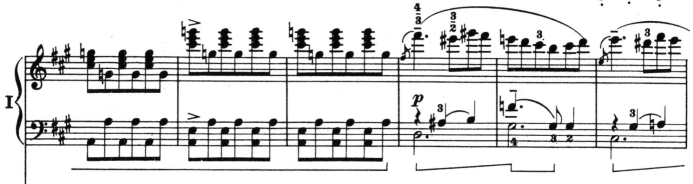

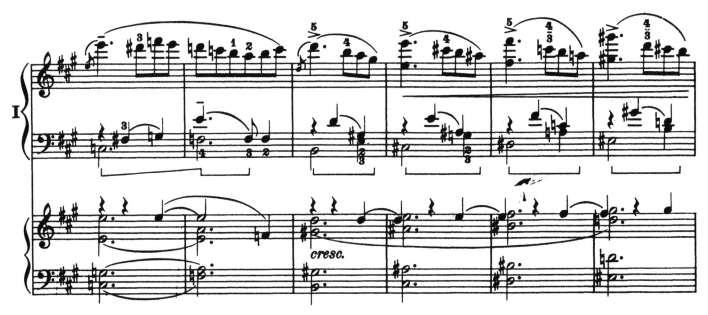

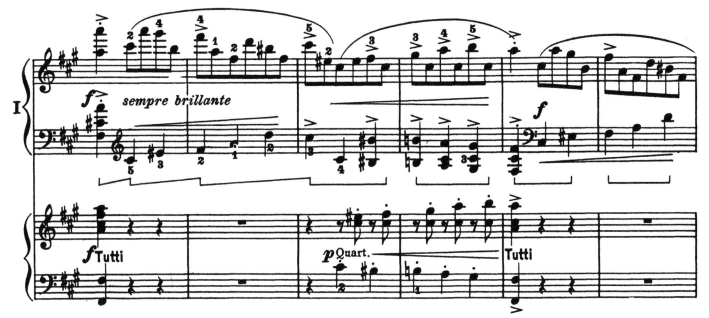

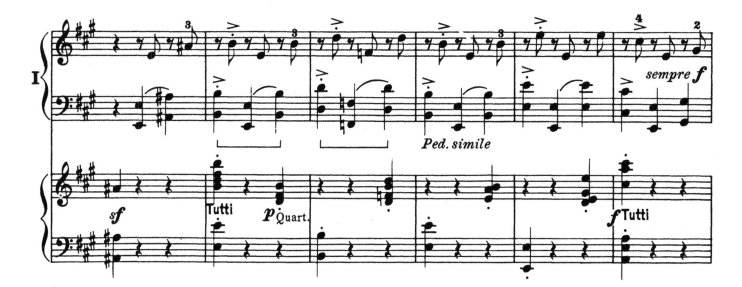